W9-AWP-180

Leaders
of
World War I

Stewart Ross

RAINTREE
STECK-VAUGHN
PUBLISHERS

A Harcourt Company

Austin   New York
www.raintreesteckvaughn.com

THE WORLD WARS

Library of Congress Cataloging-in-Publication Data
is available upon request.

ISBN 0-7398-5481-X

Printed in Hong Kong. Bound in the United States.

1 2 3 4 5 6 7 8 9 0 LB 05 04 03 02

Picture acknowledgments
AKG London 7, 18–19, 20, 24–25, 40, 48, 49, 50–51, 58–59; Camera Press 9; Hodder Wayland Picture Library 5, 12, 39; Hulton Getty 43; Mary Evans Picture Library 14; Peter Newark Historical Pictures 10, 13, 16, 21, 27, 31, 34, 37, 38, 42, 51 (top), 52, 56–57; Popperfoto 6, 11, 15, 26, 28, 29, 30, 32, 33, 35, 41, 46, 53, 54–55; Topham Picturepoint 4, 17, 22, 23, 36, 44, 45, 47.
Cover photograph: AKG London.
Field Marshal Douglas Haig, Prime Minister David Lloyd George, and Marshal Joseph Joffre.

Contents

CHAPTER ONE

Generals and Politicians

World War I—between the Allies (Britain, France, Russia, Japan, the U.S., and Italy) and the Central Powers (Germany, Austria-Hungary, and Turkey)—produced surprisingly few military commanders who caught the popular imagination. On land and sea it was a tough war of endurance. Consequently, many of its generals and admirals were themselves rather tough and unimaginative. Only in the more mobile theaters of war did heroic leaders emerge—Turkey's Mustafa Kemal in the Middle East, for example, and Germany's Paul von Lettow-Vorbeck in East Africa (see pages 52–53 and 56).

Wherever the generals fought they all shared certain characteristics. They were ambitious and forceful men who, generally, were prepared to make difficult decisions and stick to them. The better ones were good planners and communicators. And the very best—for instance, Erich von Ludendorff (Germany) and Philippe Pétain (France) (see pages 54–59 and 42–45)—had something in their characters that drew the respect and obedience of others and made them symbols of the cause for which they were fighting.

The Allied commanders—(from left to right) General Philippe Pétain (France), Field Marshal Douglas Haig (Britain), Marshal Ferdinand Foch (France), and General John Joseph Pershing (United States)—in August 1918 as they were masterminding the final Allied offensive.

The war's political leaders were an altogether more mixed group of men (no woman assumed the status of a war leader). They may be divided into two groups, the elected politicians and the hereditary heads of state (kings and emperors). The hereditary leaders included figureheads with little or no power, such as Great Britain's King George V, and all-powerful, autocratic emperors, such as Russia's Czar Nicholas II (see pages 20–23).

Elected leaders had less direct power than the politically active emperors. The power of Great Britain's prime minister, David Lloyd George (see pages 10–15), for example, rested upon the support of an elected parliament. President Woodrow Wilson (see pages 16–19) of the United States, although commander in chief of his country's armed forces, could not declare war. The U.S. Constitution gave that power to Congress. Czar Nicholas II, on the other hand, was theoretically all-powerful: He declared war, appointed ministers and generals, and personally commanded his country's forces.

Nevertheless, the war blurred the distinction between elected leaders and autocrats. Emergency regulations introduced censorship into democratic countries and even suspended democracy for a while by postponing elections. This gave men such as Britain's Lloyd George massive temporary authority. Meanwhile, hereditary rulers found that defeat and popular discontent undermined their power. Nicholas II and Germany's Kaiser Wilhelm II (see pages 24–27) were only two of several kings and emperors whose authority was smashed forever by what was known at the time as the "Great War."

"More Error Than Design"

Winston Churchill, who himself played an important role at the beginning of World War I, wondered whether any leaders really had a decisive influence on events:

"Was there any man of real eminence and responsibility whose devil heart conceived and willed this awful thing [the war]?... there is always more error than design in human affairs."

Winston Churchill, *The World Crisis, 1911–1918*, vol. 1

Ready for action? Kaiser Wilhelm II of Germany inspecting soldiers in Riga, in what is now Latvia, in September 1917. As the war dragged on, the Kaiser's political power diminished.

5

Georges Clemenceau (1841–1929)

Georges Clemenceau was 76 years old when he became prime minister of France in November 1917. Despite his age, he set about the task of rallying his war-weary country with remarkable energy and determination. Affectionately known by his fellow countrymen as "the Tiger," his inspiring leadership played an important part in holding France together during its darkest hour and enabling it to play a key role in the Allied victory a year later.

Clemenceau came from a peasant community in western France and was active in politics from the moment he went to Paris as a medical student in 1861. By 1900 he had followed a career as a doctor, journalist, writer, and fiery radical politician. Joining the government in 1906, he gained a reputation as a "strongman" prepared to make unpopular decisions—a "soldier of democracy," he called himself.

Before August 1914 Clemenceau's voice was one of the loudest calling for greater spending on armaments. As a senator, when war broke out he continued his campaign for more men and munitions and better organization and medical services. Using his newspaper *L'Homme Enchaîné* (Man in Chains), he warned against pacifism and defeatism.

Clemenceau had visited the United States as a young man, and for a while he was married to an American. He greatly admired American democracy and bombarded the U.S. with appeals to join in the

France's "Tiger," Georges Clemenceau, whose deep love of his country was born amid the pastures of his native Vendée in southwest France.

European war. When it finally did so in April 1917, he was delighted.

The impact of American power took a long time to make itself felt, and by the autumn of 1917 the morale of France and its army was at rock bottom. Victory seemed an impossible dream. In this dire situation President Raymond Poincaré turned to Clemenceau, the one man with the courage and strength to lift the nation. Insisting that "the last quarter of an hour [of the war] will be ours," Clemenceau formed a cabinet with himself as prime minister and minister of war.

Aristide Briand (1862–1932)

Like Clemenceau, Briand was a left-wing politician and journalist. He served as education minister in Clemenceau's prewar government and was prime minister at various times from 1909 to 1913. In October 1915 he became prime minister yet again, but he lacked the ruthless streak needed to lead the nation in wartime. Faced with mounting criticism of military failure and falling morale, he was forced to resign in 1917. After the war he worked hard for world peace and European unity.

Joseph Caillaux (1863–1944)

Ex-prime minister Joseph Caillaux had always been pro-German. He believed the war was pointless and should be ended as swiftly as possible. By 1917 this opinion was gaining popularity and was one reason for mutinies in the French army. In these circumstances there was an outside chance that Caillaux might become prime minister again. However, President Poincaré chose Clemenceau. Caillaux was accused of corresponding with the enemy and sent to prison.

Joseph Caillaux, the French politician whose political career was damaged when his wife shot the editor of Le Figaro newspaper in 1914 for threatening to publish love letters between her and Caillaux.

Clemenceau's contributions as a war leader were threefold. First, his powerful words lifted the nation's spirits (see panel). Second, he took almost dictatorial powers and saw that all of France's resources were employed to arrive at a single aim: victory. This involved distribution of labor, food, and resources far more strictly than before. The rigid controls were resisted, but the Tiger would allow no one to stand in his path—opponents were locked up as cowards or traitors.

Third, he insisted that the war could be won only if the Allied armies on the Western Front —French, British, and American—fought under a single, unified command.

"Solely and Utterly French"

When he became prime minister of France in November 1917, Clemenceau rallied the nation with these memorable words:

"We have one simple duty: to live with the soldier, suffer with him, fight with him. We must set aside everything that is not for the good of France. The time has come to be solely and utterly French in a way that will fill our hearts with patriotic pride."

Cited in Pierre Saulière, *Clemenceau*

The Eastern and Western Fronts during World War I.

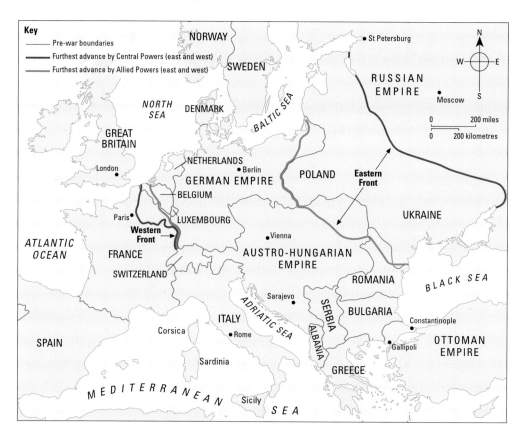

Key
— Pre-war boundaries
▬ Furthest advance by Central Powers (east and west)
▬ Furthest advance by Allied Powers (east and west)

The idea was strongly resisted but finally, in March 1918, Clemenceau had his way and France's Ferdinand Foch was appointed supreme Allied commander.

Foch stood firm in the face of Germany's last great offensive, and by the armistice of November 1918 Clemenceau's strategy had been justified. In the 1870s Prussia (the principal German state) had crushed France and seized the provinces of Alsace and Lorraine. To Clemenceau this had been a "shameful humiliation." Now, he planned for France to get its revenge.

The peacemakers, 1919. (Left to right) Italy's prime minister Vittorio Orlando, Great Britain's Lloyd George, France's Georges Clemenceau, and the U.S.'s Woodrow Wilson at the Versailles Peace Conference.

Clemenceau chaired the conference that drew up the Treaty of Versailles of June 28, 1919 (see panel). It imposed harsh terms on Germany—for example, the treaty forced Germany to pay reparations for the war damage it had caused and limited its army to 100,000 men. However, Clemenceau moderated some of his countrymen's more extreme demands, such as making Germany pay unlimited reparations.

Clemenceau's strong-arm tactics may have been necessary, but they made him many enemies. Members of the National Assembly complained that in war and peace he had ignored them and acted too much on his own initiative. Consequently, in 1920, following electoral defeat, he resigned, bringing his long and highly distinguished political career to an end.

The Treaty of Versailles

Signed in Versailles' Hall of Mirrors, where the German Empire had been proclaimed 48 years before, the Treaty of Versailles (June 28, 1919) laid down the terms of the postwar settlement in Western Europe. Germany lost several territories, including Alsace and Lorraine. Its armaments were limited and it was obliged to admit responsibility for starting the war and pay reparations (damages), but rapid inflation in the 1920s made these payments almost impossible. The Treaty also established the League of Nations, to maintain world peace and promote disarmament. The harsh terms left a legacy of bitterness in Germany.

David Lloyd George (1863–1945)

Lloyd George was Great Britain's chancellor of the exchequer. In August 1914 he was opposed to Great Britain's entry into the European war. However, after the German invasion of Belgium, he became one of the most active supporters of total war. The British nation, he declared, was "fighting for its life."

Lloyd George had never been one to avoid controversy or confrontation. As a radical Member of Parliament for Caernarvon (Wales) from 1890 and a government minister from 1905, he had opposed the South African Boer War of 1899–1902. He had pioneered important social reforms, laid the foundations of the Welfare State, and led the Liberal party's attack on the powers of the House of Lords (1909–1911). Once he was convinced that Great Britain needed to fight the European war, he threw himself into it with the same energy and intelligence that had marked his peacetime career.

Lloyd George found the army dominated by the kinds of men he had often come up against in politics—narrow-minded English (Lloyd George's first language was Welsh) conservatives from privileged backgrounds. He was critical of the military's inefficient methods of supply—failure to order replacement munitions in time, for example. He also disapproved of the tactic of trying to achieve a breakthrough on the Western Front by costly all-out assaults against heavily defended enemy positions.

The Welsh wizard: David Lloyd George, who became Great Britain's prime minister in 1916 and guided the nation through the most difficult years of the war.

At one time or another, beginning with the war minister Lord Horatio Kitchener in 1914, Lloyd George had serious disagreements with most senior British military figures. It ought to be pointed out, however, that Lloyd George's own grasp of strategy was hardly better than that of his opponents, nor did he dare veto outright battle plans of which he disapproved.

Lord Kitchener, center, with cane, whose face adorned a famous "Your Country Needs You!" poster, inspects volunteers with the Lord Mayor of London.

Lloyd George first showed his strategic innocence and lack of confidence in the military command in 1915, when he (and fellow cabinet member Winston Churchill) backed the plan to land troops at Gallipoli, in western Turkey (see page 52). The aims of the campaign were to support the Russians on the Eastern Front and force Germany and Austria to divert forces from the Western Front. Neither aim was achieved as the troops were pinned down on the coast and finally withdrawn in January 1916. By this time, Lloyd George's career had moved on.

Field Marshal Horatio Herbert Kitchener (1850–1916)

In 1914 Kitchener was a national hero—conqueror of the Sudan, victor over the Boers in South Africa, reformer of the Indian army, and ruler of Egypt. Appointed British war minister, he was one of the few to realize that the war would be long and painful. To this end he used his reputation to raise "Kitchener armies" of volunteers. However, he refused to delegate and failed to provide sufficient munitions. There was some relief among his younger colleagues, therefore, when he drowned in June 1916.

In July 1915 Prime Minister Herbert Asquith made Lloyd George minister of munitions. It was a new position, created because of the army's scandalous shortage of shells. The impact of the new minister was enormous. He cajoled business leaders, cut through red tape, and charmed the trade unions. As a result, when the British army began its major offensive on the Somme in July 1916, it did so with most of the supplies and weapons it had asked for. (Even so, the offensive was a costly disaster.)

By this time, Lloyd George's career had moved on yet again. In June 1916 he had succeeded Kitchener as war minister. By the end of the year, he had become disillusioned with the military and political conduct of the war. Only one man, he believed, had the necessary talent and drive to sort things out—himself.

Asquith was persuaded to resign on December 5, and Lloyd George replaced him as prime minister. His government, like Asquith's, contained members of all the major political parties. He reorganized the cabinet,

Women munitions workers in a factory making artillery shells. During 1915 Great Britain's shortage of munitions became a national scandal.

Herbert Henry Asquith (1852–1928)

Asquith, a highly intelligent peacetime prime minister from 1908 to 1917, lacked the spark needed by a war leader. Before 1914 he oversaw a number of reforms and controlled a lively cabinet that included Lloyd George and Winston Churchill. By late 1916, the press had undermined his reputation. Faced with a stalemate on the Western Front, severe shortages at home, and rebellion in Ireland, he was criticized for a lack of energy and imagination and forced to resign.

A great Liberal: Prime Minister H.H. Asquith in 1915. His style of leadership was perhaps too low-key for wartime.

cutting it from 23 to five members so that decisions could be made and carried out more quickly.

Lloyd George remained Great Britain's war leader for almost two years. The first of these years (1917) was grim indeed. On the battlefront he fell out with his leading commanders, William Robertson and Douglas Haig (see pages 38–41), by demanding that the Allied Spring Offensive of 1917 be under French command. It was a total failure.

This left Lloyd George with little option but to support the British offensive at the battle of Passchendaele later in the year. This, too, was a crippling disaster. By the end of the year, the prime minister was so disillusioned with Haig that he thought of trying to keep him short of troops so that he could not launch another ill-fated attack.

Sneering at Optimism

By 1917 Lloyd George had lost faith in Haig's belief in a breakthrough. The tension between the two men is quite clear in Haig's report of a meeting he had with the prime minister on June 21:

"Lloyd George made a long oration [speech], minimizing the successes gained and exaggerating the strength of the enemy....It was a regular lawyer's effort to make black appear white! He referred with a sneer to my optimistic views."

Cited in Lyn Macdonald, *They Called it Passchendaele*

During the first three years of the war, attacks on merchant vessels by Germany's U-boats proved a highly effective way of preventing supplies from reaching Great Britain from the United States. Here, the crew of a torpedoed British ship take to their lifeboats.

Not all the news was grim. In 1917 Lloyd George had backed the idea of convoys to cut the number of merchant ships being sunk by enemy submarines. The measure was a success and ensured that Great Britain's vital supply lines remained open for the rest of the war.

Along with Georges Clemenceau (see pages 6–9), Lloyd George had long called for a unified Allied military command. Haig had constantly rejected the idea. Lloyd George finally had his way after the first successes of the German Spring Offensive. In March 1918 Marshal Ferdinand Foch (see pages 32–37) was appointed to oversee and direct all Allied strategy.

After the armistice (November 1918), Lloyd George, with the support of the Conservative party, continued the coalition government. He won the election of December 1918 and, steering a middle course between the United States and France, played a key role in drawing up the postwar 1919 Treaty of Versailles (see page 9).

However, by 1920 many politicians were losing patience with Lloyd George. Too often, it seemed, the whiff of political and sexual scandal hung about him (see panel), nor could he be trusted, brilliant though he might be. Finally, in the autumn of 1922, Conservatives in Parliament refused to support him any longer and he resigned his office.

The Labour party and the Liberals who had supported Asquith had already ceased to back Lloyd George. Left at the head of a shrinking and divided Liberal party, Lloyd George entered the political wilderness. Although he remained a MP (Member of Parliament) until the year of his death, he never again held government office.

Scandal

Lloyd George had many fine qualities —insight, charm, the power to persuade, and a genuine wish to help the less fortunate. However, on occasion he could be devious. Twice (1913 and 1922) he was involved in major financial scandals. Colleagues disliked his love of plotting, as, for example, when he arranged privately for a French general, Nivelle (see page 34), to lead the 1917 Offensive. Respectable politicians were shocked by his private life, too. His wife chose to live in the family home in North Wales, while he lived with his mistress in London.

Victory parade—survivors of the most costly war ever fought march through the streets of London, July 1919. Lloyd George was a highly respected wartime leader, but his postwar popularity soon waned.

Woodrow Wilson, the 28th U.S. president. He was the only occupant of the White House to have had an academic career.

President Woodrow Wilson

In some ways Woodrow Wilson (1856–1924) was the most unusual war leader. He was an idealistic scholar rather than a soldier, the first and only professional academic ever to become U.S. president. More than any other major wartime figure, he was an idealist who had a clear vision of a better world.

Elected president of the United States in 1912, Wilson and his Democratic party introduced a program of sweeping and successful reform. As a child he had witnessed firsthand the horrors of the American Civil War (1861–1865), and when war came to Europe in 1914 he was eager to keep the United States neutral. This policy was tested in 1915 and 1916, when Germany introduced "unrestricted" submarine warfare, sinking with torpedoes ships suspected of trading with its enemies. Wilson was reelected in 1916 on the slogan, "He kept us out of the war."

Shortly after his reelection, Wilson launched a vigorous campaign for "peace without victory" in Europe. He offered the United States as a mediator and a League of Nations to ensure peace in the future. There were even vague threats of using U.S. force to bring the warring sides to a peace conference. All these strategies were hopelessly unrealistic, and Europeans dismissed them out of hand.

Germany, which had stopped its unrestricted submarine warfare in 1916, reopened it in February 1917. Meanwhile, the Germans had approached Mexico as a potential ally (see panel). This tactless aggression forced Wilson's hand. With great sorrow, in April 1917 he asked Congress to declare war on Germany. His request was granted. Unlike the leaders of most of the other warring nations, he entered the war with reluctance. He had, he believed, been left with no choice. But now that America was involved, he wanted to use its power to bring the conflict to a swift conclusion and build a better world on the ruins of the old.

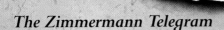

The Zimmermann Telegram

In January 1917 the German foreign minister, Arthur Zimmermann, sent a secret message to a German diplomat in Mexico. It said that if Mexico joined the Central Powers, it might take over part of the southern United States. The British intercepted the telegram and passed it on to the U.S. government. When the press was told of its contents, war fever gripped the country. A month later (April 6, 1917), the U.S. formally declared war on Germany.

Wilson's campaign posters, 1916. The following April the man who "Keeps Us Out of War" led the U.S. into World War I on the side of the Allies.

Surprisingly, Wilson turned out to be a good war leader. He took a close interest in what was going on but delegated to experts where necessary. For example, he appointed General John J. Pershing (see page 37) to command the American Expeditionary Force (AEF) in Europe and made sure that he was well supplied with troops and munitions. By the end of the war there were some two million American men and women in Europe, and U.S. forces played a small but significant role in the victorious Allied advance that began in the summer of 1918.

By this time Wilson was concentrating on bringing about a just and lasting peace. As a basis for this, in January 1918 he put forward fourteen points. One of his principal

The Fourteen Points

The speech in which Wilson introduced his fourteen points to Congress on January 8, 1918, is one of the most idealistic ever made by a world statesman in modern times:

"The day of conquest and aggrandizement [power grabbing] *is gone by.... We demand...that the world be made safe and fit to live in; and particularly that it be made safe for every peace-loving nation which, like our own, wishes to live its own life.... The program of the world's peace, therefore, is our program...."*

Hofstadter, *Great Issues in American History,* vol. 2

suggestions—peace without blame—was rejected by the Versailles Peace Conference of 1919. Instead, the Treaty of Versailles punished Germany as the nation most responsible for starting and continuing the war. However, Wilson's second big idea—a League of Nations to preserve peace and resolve international conflict—was widely acclaimed and accepted. But not, alas, in the United States.

The U.S. Constitution states that to be valid all treaties have to be signed by the president and accepted by a two-thirds majority of the Senate. Back home after attending the Versailles Conference, the exhausted Wilson campaigned to convince the American people to accept the Treaty and, more specifically, the idea of the League. The strain was too much for him. He had a serious stroke in October 1919, and the Senate rejected the Treaty of Versailles (1919 and 1920). A separate U.S. agreement ended the war with Germany in 1921. The United States never joined the League of Nations. Although Wilson made some recovery from his illness, his judgment was impaired. He was defeated in the 1920 election and died three years later.

Action at last—U.S. troops engage the enemy in the Argonne Forest, September 1918. By this time U.S. General Pershing had molded his army of raw recruits into an effective fighting force.

CHAPTER THREE

The Emperors

Czar Nicholas II (1868–1918)

Russia's last czar, Nicholas II (ruled 1894–1917), was the most powerful of all Europe's hereditary rulers. Unfortunately, his power was not matched by his ability. The strains of World War I destroyed Russia's ancient system of government and cost the lives of the czar and his family, as well as millions of their subjects.

There were plenty of signs before the outbreak of war in 1914 that Nicholas was ill-suited to the task of leading and governing a vast empire of some 170 million people. Defeat by Japan in the Russo-Japanese War of 1904–1905 had led to a revolution in Russia (1905) that forced the czar to set up a parliament, the Duma. The czar later backtracked on his promises of reform, angering the country's many opposition groups and leading to calls for further change.

Nicholas would not budge. He believed that God had made him czar and given him autocratic powers over his empire. His obstinacy blinded him to his own unpopularity and, especially, to that of his German-born wife. Her close relationship with Rasputin, the supposed holy man who claimed to help her son's hemophilia, was a major scandal.

On the outbreak of war, Nicholas' popularity temporarily soared. As the "Little Father" of his people, he would lead them to glorious victory —just as his ancestor Alexander I had done in 1813. (The forces of Czar Alexander had played a major part in the defeat of the French

Scandal at court: A Russian cartoon showing the czar and his wife, Alexandra, wholly in the grip of the mystical but corrupt "holy man," Gregory Rasputin.

emperor Napoleon I after he had unsuccessfully invaded Russia.) The reality of 1914 was somewhat different.

The massive Russian army was regarded as a "steamroller"—slow to get moving but unstoppable once it had built up speed. In fact, the Russians advanced into Germany more quickly than expected but were shatteringly defeated at Tannenberg (August 1914) and Masurian Lakes (September 1914). By the end of the year, military defeat and the government's inability to organize the war had completely dissolved the country's feelings of loyalty and optimism.

The Russian experience illustrates how differently democratic and autocratic nations dealt with leadership difficulties brought on by war. When dissatisfaction built up with Prime Minister Herbert Asquith in Great Britain, for example, he was replaced by a colleague, David Lloyd George. This was done within the system of government, not by changing the system. This was impossible in Russia, because the czar *was* the system of government. Everything that went wrong was laid at his door. Since he was theoretically irreplaceable, when things went wrong there was no option but revolution.

The "Little Father" of the Russian Empire, Czar Nicholas II, holds a religious picture before his kneeling troops. In the end, the czar's semi-religious status did not save him from abdication and murder.

Nicholas made matters worse by appointing ministers of generally poor quality and then quickly dismissing them when they proved incompetent. A good example was the dim-witted General Vladimir Sukhomilov, Russia's minister of war in August 1914. Heavily in debt, Sukhomilov was befriended by a German spy, Fritz Helmer. The spy helped the general with his financial problems—and picked up plenty of useful military information in the process. Meanwhile, to add a dash of spice to the story, the spy was also having an affair with the general's wife.

Not surprisingly, with incompetent men such as these at the helm, Russia ground to a halt. The railroad system—essential for moving men, munitions, and food—collapsed through lack of maintenance. Soldiers were sent to the front unarmed and told to collect weapons from fallen colleagues. Perhaps most absurd of all, in August 1915 the czar took personal command of the Russian armies. Not only did he have no relevant military training, but being at the front cut him off from the deteriorating situation at home.

Transport chaos! Scenes like this, in which thousands of disorganized troops try to board an overcrowded train, were common in Russia as the railroad system collapsed in 1916. Ultimate responsibility for the failure rested with the czar.

"Supreme Command"

In a letter to Grand Duke Nicholas, the Russian commander in chief at the start of the war, the czar announced his intention of taking over personal command of his armies:

"Now that the enemy has penetrated far into the Empire, my duty to the country that God has committed to my keeping ordains [orders] that I shall assume supreme command of the fighting forces, share the burdens and toils of war with my army, and help it to protect Russian soil against the onslaught of the foes."

Cited in Robert K. Massie, *Nicholas and Alexandra*

In 1916 improved supplies enabled General Brusilov (see pages 28–31) to launch a moderately successful offensive against Austria-Hungary. This did not save the czar or his autocracy, however. Military deaths now exceeded one million. By the beginning of 1917, supplies of food and fuel to the major cities had almost dried up. Millions faced starvation. Nicholas had lost the support of the entire nation.

No leader could carry on in such circumstances. A revolution overthrew the czar and his government in March 1917 and established a provisional government. Perhaps unwisely, this provisional government continued the war and in November was itself overthrown, this time in a communist revolution. Nicholas and his family were imprisoned and moved to Siberia, where they were murdered in 1918.

Russian soldiers on the Eastern Front. The czar completely failed to inspire trust in his troops, despite his own belief in his military abilities.

Kaiser Wilhelm II

Of all the World War I leaders, Germany's Wilhelm II (ruled 1888–1918) was perhaps the most complicated. He was intelligent but occasionally rash. In 1908, for example, he damaged Anglo-German relations by telling the British *Daily Telegraph* that many Germans were anti-English. He was torn between trying to be a liberal gentleman (the wish of his English mother, a daughter of Queen Victoria) and a traditional iron-willed Prussian warrior-king. This latter role was unrealistic because he had a damaged left arm that never grew to its normal size. Some historians believe this caused him to suffer from a painful inferiority complex.

Calm before the storm: Germany's Kaiser Wilhelm II (center) with his family on board their royal yacht, 1913.

Der Kaiser, Prinz Adalbert, Prinzessin Viktoria Luise und die Kronprinzessin mit den Prinzen Wilhelm, Louis Ferdinand und Hubertus.

Emperor Franz Josif (1830–1916)

Coming to the Austrian throne in 1848 and accepting the crown of Hungary in 1867, Franz Josif struggled for the rest of his life to hold the scattered Dual Monarchy together. He began the Great War by seeking to destroy Serbia. Two years later, dependent upon Germany for his empire's survival, he declared on his deathbed, "I took over the throne under the most difficult conditions, and I am leaving it under even worse ones."

Wilhelm's life was not made easier by his unclear and tricky position as kaiser (emperor) of Germany. The German Empire and its constitution had been in existence only since 1871. The emperor's power appeared very great: He could appoint and dismiss the chancellor (prime minister) and he commanded the army and navy. However, the chancellor had to have the support of the elected Reichstag (parliament), which oversaw financial matters. Furthermore, everyday control over the armed forces was exercised by professional officers.

All this made Wilhelm's situation difficult. He was not just a figurehead, like his cousin George V of the British Empire. On the other hand, although he was expected to lead, he did not have the real powers of, say, Russia's Nicholas II. Nevertheless, Wilhelm still had enormous influence. His personal tragedy—and that of the entire world—is that he did not exercise this influence more wisely. He posed as a great and powerful leader but did not have the will to exercise such leadership, nor did he appoint those who might have done so on his behalf.

"A Just Defense"

In August 1914, after Germany had declared war on Russia, Emperor Wilhelm II put on his military uniform and addressed an enthusiastic Berlin crowd:

"A fateful hour has fallen upon Germany. Envious people on all sides are compelling us to resort to a just defense. The sword is being forced into our hands....And now I command you to go to church, kneel before God, and pray to him help our gallant army."

Cited in John Keegan, *The First World War*

One example of Wilhelm's uncertain and unfortunate influence was his appointment, in 1909, of Theobald von Bethmann Hollweg as chancellor. Bethmann Hollweg remained in power until 1917. He disliked working with the Reichstag, so his government was continually short of money. This made it difficult to keep up in the arms race with Great Britain, France, and Russia. This feeling of lagging behind militarily was one reason for the chancellor's backing the emperor's "blank check" for Austria-Hungary in July 1914 (see page 27). The sooner war came, Bethmann Hollweg and the German chiefs of staff argued, the better would be their chance of victory.

German vice chancellor Karl Helfferich (right) talks with Chancellor Bethmann Hollweg (in uniform) in June 1914. Foreign secretary Gottlieb von Jagow (center) listens in.

Assassination at Sarajevo

On June 28, 1914, Archduke Franz Ferdinand, heir to the throne of Austria-Hungary, visited Sarajevo, the principal town of Bosnia-Herzegovina. Austria's annexation of these provinces in 1908 had been deeply resented by neighboring Serbia. During the archduke's visit he and his wife were assassinated by Gavrilo Princip, a young Bosnian who belonged to an anti-Austrian gang with Serbian backing. Austria swiftly discovered the Serbian link. Austria's reaction to the assassination started a train of events that soon led to world war.

The Blank Check

After the assassination of Archduke Franz Ferdinand, Wilhelm II promised to back Austria-Hungary in whatever action it decided to take. For this "blank check" offer of support, Wilhelm has sometimes been held personally responsible for the outbreak of World War I. This is probably unfair. He imagined war, certainly, but only a limited and short one. He had no idea that his promise would spark a worldwide conflict of horrific magnitude.

Once the war had begun, Wilhelm's influence declined. He made formal appearances at parades and so forth, and made warlike pronouncements on a future victory. As supreme commander in chief, he dismissed generals Moltke (1914) (see page 54) and Falkenhayn (1916) (see page 48). Increasingly, however, he left day-to-day military decisions to his favored commanders. He particularly approved of Paul von Hindenburg (see pages 48–51), one of the heroes of the great victory over the Russians at Tannenberg (see page 48).

Hindenburg was a general bent on victory at all costs. By the end of 1916, with casualties mounting alarmingly, it was becoming clear that victory of any sort was remote, even unlikely. At that moment, perhaps, with U.S. president Wilson offering to mediate, Wilhelm might have overridden his generals and explored the possibility of an honorable peace. He did not do so.

Instead, Wilhelm gave enough power to generals Hindenburg and Erich von Ludendorff (see pages 54–59) that they became virtual rulers of Germany. Finally, in 1918, when defeat was certain, it took Wilhelm a long time to realize that his time as emperor was over, too. He eventually abdicated, under pressure, on November 9 and fled to the Netherlands. Calls for him to be returned and tried as a war criminal came to nothing, and he lived abroad as a country gentleman until his death in 1941.

One of the lucky ones? A German prisoner of war, depressed but uninjured, at the end of 1916. By this time even Hindenburg was aware that the defeat of the Central Powers was likely.

CHAPTER FOUR

The Allied Commanders

General Aleksey Brusilov (1853–1926)

Aleksey Brusilov, of Russia, was unlike most of World War I's successful military commanders. Where they made names for themselves by painstaking preparation and planning, rarely taking risks, he showed unusual flair and daring. Indeed, the success his military leadership brought in 1916 may have altered the course of the war by saving his ally France from defeat.

The lively, energetic Brusilov was born in Tiflis, Georgia. He was from a well-connected family, and trained as a cavalry officer in the imperial army. This, and his supreme self-confidence, may explain his liking for campaigns of attack and movement. He made a name for himself in Russia's brief war with Turkey (1877–1878), and in 1914 he was the general commanding the Russian Eighth Army in Galicia, in central Europe. He played an important role in Russia's spectacular capture of Galicia from Austria-Hungary at the end of 1914.

General Brusilov, one of Czar Nicholas II's few really talented generals.

General Alexander Samsonov (1859–1914)

Samsonov was a general of the old school. He had fought in the Russo-Japanese War of 1904–1905 and had served as governor of Turkestan. In 1914 he commanded the Russian Second Army that advanced into Prussia alongside the First Army under General Rennenkampf. The two generals strongly disliked each other. Their failure to cooperate led to Samsonov's isolation and defeat at Tannenberg (August 29). In despair, he fled into the woods and shot himself.

Russian infantry set out for the front to engage in the battle for Poland. The Central Powers had gained control of Poland by winter 1915.

The following year, Germany came to the rescue of her Austro-Hungarian ally. General Hindenburg (see pages 48–51) launched a massive counteroffensive on the central sector of the Russian front. Brusilov, whose Eighth Army was based farther south, could do little to resist the German offensive. However, it was partly due to his counterattack that the German advance was finally halted. By the time winter set in, the Russians had lost Galicia and Poland.

General Nikolay Yudenich (1862–1933)

A small but important battlefront divided the Russian and Turkish empires across the Caucasuses. Here, between 1914 and 1916, the Russian general Nikolay Yudenich fought with considerable success. He helped push back a Turkish invasion at the start of the war and replied with a powerful counteroffensive of his own in 1916. After the communist revolution of November 1917, he fought against the Red Army in northwest Russia, before fleeing to exile in France in 1920.

The scene was now set for Brusilov's finest moment. In March 1916 the czar appointed him to command all the Russian forces on the Southwestern Front. Shortly afterward, Nicholas II responded to desperate appeals from his French and Italian allies, and agreed to a new offensive. Brusilov chose his target carefully, attacking the Austrian rather than the German sectors of the line. He also decided upon a new surprise tactic: Instead of concentrating his attack on a narrow section of the enemy front line, in June he ordered an attack along a massive 300-mile (480-km) front.

Taken by surprise, the Austrian front line was pierced and its troops fell back with heavy losses. By September, three separate Russian offensives had brought advances of more than 50 miles (80 km) along the entire front. Hundreds of thousands of the enemy had been killed or wounded and 375,000 taken prisoner.

More important, Austria-Hungary had been forced to move men from the Italian Front to reinforce its retreating line. This took the strain off the hard-pressed Italians. Brusilov's success had also forced the German chief of staff General Falkenhayn (see page 48) to withdraw troops from an assault on Verdun on the Western Front. This greatly helped the French, who had been close to defeat. Finally, seeing the spectacular Russian success, in August 1916 Romania joined the war on the side of the Allies.

Nevertheless, the Brusilov Offensive had serious consequences for Russia, too. Huge losses further undermined the army's morale. Brusilov himself became disillusioned with the czar's leadership. His offensive had been severely hampered by the inefficiency of the Russian railroad system and a frustrating shortage of munitions. The responsibility for both of these shortcomings lay ultimately with the czar.

Vladimir Ulyanov I. Lenin (1870–1924)

Lenin led the Bolshevik (communist) party that toppled Russia's provisional government in November 1917. He had been in exile in Switzerland for most of the war but returned to Russia (with German help) after the revolution of February 1917. Forced to flee to Finland in the summer of 1917, he returned to Russia at the outbreak of the November revolution. Realizing better than any other leader how unpopular the war had become, he made "peace" the first word of his revolutionary slogan: "Peace, Bread, Land." However, Russia could not simply stop fighting, and a treaty was not signed with Germany until March 1918. By this time, Lenin had assumed great personal power, making him a sort of "communist czar."

Leon Bronstein Trotsky (1879–1940)

When Lenin (see panel opposite) reached Petrograd (St. Petersburg) in November 1917, the city was already in communist hands. This was the work of Leon Trotsky. As foreign commissar, Trotsky opened peace negotiations with the Germans (1917–1918) at Brest-Litovsk, accepting Germany's terms after further Russian defeats in 1918. Having reorganized the Red Army and masterminded the communist victory in the Civil War (1918–1921), he opposed Lenin's successor, Joseph Stalin, and was exiled in 1929.

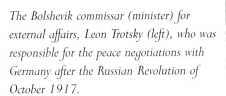

The Bolshevik commissar (minister) for external affairs, Leon Trotsky (left), who was responsible for the peace negotiations with Germany after the Russian Revolution of October 1917.

In March 1917 Brusilov was one of the leading generals who advised Nicholas II to abdicate. Shortly afterward, the Provisional Government of March–November 1917 appointed him Russia's new commander in chief. He launched a fresh offensive in the summer of 1917 but, as before, after initial advances his men floundered in the face of well-organized German resistance. Brusilov was dismissed in July 1917.

Unlike many ex-czarist generals, Brusilov did not leave Russia after the communist revolution of November 1917. Instead, he joined the Red (communist) Army in 1920 and served as a military consultant until retiring in 1924.

Ferdinand Foch, the French general who masterminded the Allied advance to victory on the Western Front, from July to November 1918.

Marshal Ferdinand Foch (1851–1929)

Ferdinand Foch (pronounced "Fosh") was one of the few military commanders to emerge at the end of World War I with his reputation undamaged. In addition, he had achieved a lifetime's ambition: winning back his homeland, Lorraine, which had been lost to Germany 48 years earlier.

Foch came from eastern France, and in 1869 he entered a Jesuit school in Metz, a fortress city in the region of Lorraine. After France's humiliating defeat in the Franco-Prussian War (1870–1871), Lorraine was absorbed into the new German Empire and Foch found himself living alongside German soldiers. The experience scarred him badly and bred in him a strong thirst for revenge.

After joining the army in 1873, Foch became well known as a first-class military thinker. He was at the French War College on three separate occasions, serving as its head in 1908. His two books—*The Principles of War* (1903) and *On the Conduct of War* (1904) —were widely read and respected.

When war broke out in 1914, the 63-year-old Foch commanded an army corps on the frontier with Lorraine. Always eager to attack, Foch's first movement was forward. He then fell back and skilfully defended the city of Nancy. By this action he proved his worth as a practical soldier as well as a theoretical one.

Marshal Joseph Jacques Césaire Joffre (1852–1931)

As chief of the general staff, Joffre had drawn up France's battle plan for war with Germany. However, his "Plan XVII" failed and he had to reorganize swiftly to save Paris. This he achieved at the Battle of the Marne (September 1914), which made him a national hero. Two years of grinding attrition and catastrophic losses tarnished his golden reputation, and he was eventually replaced by General Nivelle (see page 34) at the end of 1916. He was given a position of suitable prestige, but played no further active part in the conduct of the war.

The savior of France at the Battle of the Marne, 1914, Marshal Joseph Joffre was removed from battle command at the end of 1916 after two years of seemingly hopeless slaughter.

The French chief of staff, Marshal Joseph Joffre (see panel), recognized Foch's talent and put him in charge of a new Ninth Army. In this command Foch played a key part in the Battle of the Marne (September 1914), the action that finally halted the German attack on Paris. Foch then worked closely with the British and the Belgians in the "race to the sea"—the extension of the front line to the Channel to keep the Allies from being outflanked. The experience of working closely with forces of other nations was to prove invaluable to Foch in the last year of the war.

Plan XVII

Marshal Joffre produced "Plan XVII" in April 1913. He believed the main German attack would drive west, through Alsace and Lorraine. To counter this, Joffre planned a two-pronged attack in the opposite direction. When war came, the French moved east but ran into fierce German resistance. Meanwhile, the main German attack came from the northwest, through Belgium. When he realized what was happening, Joffre quickly abandoned Plan XVII and hurried to defend Paris.

For most of 1915 and 1916 Foch was stuck on the northern sector of the French line, planning and carrying out fruitless attacks against heavily defended German positions. This static warfare was not to his liking and his reputation suffered, particularly with the costly failure of the Somme offensive in the summer of 1916. Finally, when Joffre was dismissed as commander in chief in December 1916, Foch was moved from frontline command to take up an advisory post.

Mutiny man: the costly failure of Marshal Robert Nivelle's offensive in the spring of 1917 led to widespread mutinies and the prompt removal of the commander in chief.

Marshal Robert Nivelle (1856–1924)

Nivelle's reputation rested on his invention of the "creeping barrage"—troops advancing behind a sweeping carpet of artillery fire. After the tactic brought success at Verdun, in 1916 Nivelle was appointed French commander in chief in place of Joffre. Nivelle was one of the old school of French marshals who believed that attack was the best means of defense. He explained this to the men of the Second Army in 1916:

"… you must not be content with resistance. By continued and incessant pressure on the enemy, you must force him to keep in line against you as many of his troops as you can hold there, until the hour strikes, as it will soon, for the general offensive."

Cited in David Mason, Verdun

Nivelle's reputation and career were destroyed the following spring when, as many had predicted, yet another massive French offensive ended in ghastly casualties and minuscule gains. Nivelle spent the rest of the war in North Africa.

Foch was not a man to be put down. During the Battle of the Marne, for example, he had reported, "I am hard pressed on my right; my center is giving way; situation excellent; I am attacking." Clemenceau had the sense to realize that a man with a spirit like this had to be used, and in May 1917 Foch was appointed advisor to the Allied armies. In this position he helped reorganize the Italian army after its disastrous defeat at Caporetto (October 1917). While engaged on this work, Foch was confirmed in his view that the Allies would be an effective fighting force only when they acted under a single, supreme command. For the time being, neither Lloyd George nor Clemenceau would listen.

In the spring of 1918, as Foch had predicted, the Germans moved huge resources from the Eastern Front and launched one massive last offensive. Masterminded by General Ludendorff (see pages 54–59), the attack came very close to success. By late March the British were thinking of withdrawal across the Channel, and Marshal Philippe Pétain was wondering how he might defend Paris. At this point Clemenceau agreed to Lloyd George's suggestion that Foch be asked to coordinate the Allies' efforts. Coordination soon turned into control.

Field Marshal Armando Diaz (1861–1928)

The cautious Diaz witnessed Italy's successes on its northern frontier at Carso and Gorizia (August 1916). He replaced Field Marshal Luigi Cadorna (1850–1928) as Italian chief of staff after the crushing defeat at Caporetto (October 1917) and used his excellent leadership skills to rebuild the morale of the Italian army. Avoiding an offensive until he was sure of success, he destroyed the crumbling Austrians at Vittorio Veneto (October–November 1918) and was proclaimed "Duke of Victory."

Italy's élite—men of the "Alpini" (Alpine) corps—were experienced in mountain warfare. Foch's work with the Italian army helped persuade him that the Allies should operate under a single command.

As supreme commander of the Allied forces, Foch's tactic was to soak up German pressure and wait for the right moment to counterattack. He cleverly moved men and equipment by road and rail to where they were needed most, plugging gaps in the line when it looked as if Ludendorff might burst through. Eventually, in mid-July, the German offensive burned itself out. Foch immediately ordered a counterattack, before the enemy had time to recover.

The first Allied offensive came in July; the second in August. The Amiens Offensive (August 8–September 4, 1918) was perhaps Foch's finest achievement. After a brief artillery bombardment, Allied forces advanced along a 14-mile (22-km) front, supported by hundreds of tanks and aircraft. By the end of Day One (which Ludendorff called "the Black Day of the German army") the Allies had advanced up to 10 miles (16 km). After years of stalemate, it was a remarkable achievement. In some places German troops had fled the battlefield and thousands of prisoners had been taken. By the time the offensive ended, Ludendorff realized the war was lost.

American troops in Meuse, 1918. U.S. forces and armaments were key factors in the success of the Meuse-Argonne offensive.

Later in September the Americans broke through at St. Mihiel before Foch launched the final Meuse-Argonne Offensive, which lasted from September 26 to November 11, 1918. By now huge numbers of American troops had arrived and were sufficiently experienced to play an important part in operations. Faced with Foch, Haig (see pages 38–41), and Pershing (see panel opposite) working closely together, the Germans were forced to retreat along the line and finally accepted a cease-fire on November 11.

General John Joseph Pershing (1860–1948)

Pershing, known as "Black Jack" (a nickname he collected when serving with an African-American regiment early in his career), commanded the AEF from 1917–1919. Before arriving in France, having fought in the Indian Wars and the Philippines and chased bandits in Mexico, he had no experience of large-scale modern warfare. Nevertheless, he soon grasped the complexity and enormity of the task he faced. He sent home for an extra two million troops and began shaping his men into an effective fighting force. He also learned the need to cooperate with the French and British. Not surprisingly, at first the dour Pershing showed little flair as a battlefield commander. He learned from experience, however, and by October 1918 U.S. forces were spearheading parts of the Allied advance. They performed particularly well at St. Mihiel (September 1918). Two weeks later, when they failed to impress in the Argonne Forest, Clemenceau asked that Pershing be dismissed. The call was refused and after a successful last few weeks of the war, the American general returned home to be rewarded with the unique rank "general of the armies."

General Pershing (third from right) arrives in Boulogne, France, in June 1917.

Being made a field marshal of the British army was only one of the many honors heaped upon Foch after the war. He was even invited to attend the Versailles Peace Conference, where he saw that his beloved Lorraine was returned to France, although his bitter calls for even harsher terms for Germany were not heeded.

Field Marshal Douglas Haig (1861–1928)

Douglas Haig was a most controversial war leader. He had many fine qualities. He was tough and determined, and in open battle he proved a skilled tactician. He was able to win the loyalty of the men he commanded, and he learned to adapt to changing circumstances. Against this must be set his inflexibility and his apparent insensitivity to loss and suffering, the suspicion that he was helped by his contacts in high places (including King George V), and his slowness in recognizing a changing military situation.

Haig, who was the British commander in chief from 1915 to 1918, is closely associated with three terrible offensives: the Somme in 1916, and, in 1917, Arras and the Third Battle of Ypres (also known as the Battle of Passchendaele).

General Sir William Robertson (1860–1933)

Robertson rose from the ranks (he did not enter the army as an officer) to take over supply of the British Expeditionary Force in 1914. Early the next year he became the army's chief of staff. In December 1915 he was called back from France and promoted to be chief of the imperial general staff. In this position he was the principal military advisor to the British cabinet. Like Haig, he believed that the only way to defeat Germany was to wear it down by a war of attrition on the Western Front. This brought him into conflict with Lloyd George, who dismissed him in February 1918. He was given a home appointment until 1919, when he took over command of the British army occupying the Rhine area of Germany.

Sir Douglas Haig commanded the British army in France from 1915 until 1918. His gritty strategy was, and still is, a source of much contention.

Each resulted in gigantic losses and minimal gains on the ground. In short, they may be regarded as pointless slaughter that Haig should have called off when he saw that no progress was being made.

On the other hand, Haig was no different from most other commanders of the time, such as Joffre or Falkenhayn (see page 48). The Western Front was no place for the fainthearted. In a war of attrition, the winner is the commander whose resolve never falters. Haig, his defenders suggest, was just such a man. In his most famous order (April 12, 1918) he wrote: "There must be no retirement. With our backs to the wall and believing in the justice of our cause each one must fight on to the end." Furthermore, it may be argued, although the Somme, Arras, and Third Ypres captured little territory, they took pressure off the faltering French army. They also ground the Germans down, so that when they in turn attempted an offensive (spring 1918), it too failed.

Like many British soldiers, Haig's early military career was spent abroad. He served in the Sudan, South Africa, and India (hardly ideal preparation for the Western Front), before taking command of part of the British Expeditionary Force (BEF) headquartered at the Aldershot military base in southern England. At this time, incidentally, Haig described the machine gun as "a much overrated weapon." Going to France in August 1914, he distinguished himself by the way he handled his troops at the First Battle of Ypres (October–November 1914).

T. E. (Thomas Edward) Lawrence (1888–1935)

"Lawrence of Arabia" became a favorite of the British public, although his reputation rests on uncertain foundations. In love with Arabia and the Arab people, in 1916 he joined guerrillas operating behind the Turkish lines. At that time most Arab peoples were in revolt against the Turkish Empire, the controlling power in the Middle East. Leading by example, Lawrence seems to have inspired the Arabs in their revolt. His daring exploits assisted the more formal military campaign that General Allenby was waging against the Turks. Lawrence's promises of an independent Arab nation were betrayed by Western politicians, and he spent the rest of his life fleeing publicity and adding to the growing legend about himself.

Haig became a general in 1915 and soon found himself in disagreement with his commander in chief, Sir John French. He communicated his doubts about French's competence in letters to the king. When French was dismissed in December 1915, Haig took his place. He remained commander in chief of the British army for the duration of the war.

Haig believed that the war could be won only by a breakthrough on the Western Front. Unlike many, he thought such a breakthrough

Field Marshal Douglas Haig (second from left) addresses a skeptical David Lloyd George (right) before the Allied offensive on the Somme, 1916. Marshal Joseph Joffre (center) seems about to intervene on Haig's side.

"I Felt It My Duty"

When war broke out, Haig admitted in his diary that he had criticized Sir John French to the king:

"I told him [King George V] *at once, as I felt it was my duty to do so, that…I had grave doubts…whether either* [French's] *temper was sufficiently even or his military knowledge sufficiently thorough to enable him to discharge properly the very difficult duties which will devolve upon him during the coming operations. …In my own heart, I know that French is quite unfit for this great command at a time of crisis in our Nation's history."*

Haig's diary, cited in Lyn Macdonald, ed., *1914–1918 Voices and Images of the Great War*

Admiral Sir John Jellicoe (1859–1935)

John Jellicoe was highly intelligent, popular, and diligent. He rose fast to command the British Grand Fleet in 1914. When the expected confrontation with the German High Seas Fleet came at Jutland in May 1916, Jellicoe won a strategic victory but suffered heavy losses and missed the opportunity to press home his advantage. Criticized by Lloyd George as "tired and over-conscientious," he was dismissed in December 1917. After the war he served as governor of New Zealand.

possible and, as noted above, attempted it on several occasions in 1916 and 1917. The front line advanced only about 6 miles (10 km) on the Somme at the cost of 419,000 casualties. Similar gains were made at Arras with the loss of 150,000 men. The story was the same at Ypres, where the casualties totaled 310,000.

By the end of 1917, Prime Minister Lloyd George wished to dismiss Haig. He did not do so, partly for fear of the pessimistic signal this would send to the country—a fired commander would imply that the vast number of casualties had been in vain. Instead, Lloyd George urged Haig not to launch yet another costly offensive.

In 1918 Haig willingly accepted Marshal Ferdinand Foch as the overall Allied commander. In the spring and early summer, he rebuilt his shattered army. Then, starting at Amiens on August 8, he directed a series of nine successful offensives. These were very important achievements and led to the eventual Allied victory. They did not, however, erase the memory of the dreadful slaughter of the previous two years.

Admiral Lord Jellicoe was the only man who, in the words of Winston Churchill, could in theory lose the war in a day— by allowing the enemy to destroy Britain's Grand Fleet.

Marshal Philippe Pétain (1856–1951)

Few men have had such a tragically roller-coaster career as Philippe Pétain. An able student from an undistinguished background, he won a place at France's leading military academy. Then, after some experience with an Alpine regiment (specializing in mountain warfare), he returned to the war college as a lecturer. Here he challenged the popular French strategy— *attaque à l'outrance* (attack to the bitter end).

Pétain explained that an all-out attack was suicide against breech-loading rifles, machine guns, artillery, and barbed wire. As evidence he pointed to the slaughter in the American Civil War (1861–1865) and the Russo-Japanese War (1904–1905). An offensive, Pétain believed, could take place only after the enemy's defenses had been severely weakened by artillery fire. History, of course, was to prove him right. But at the time these unorthodox views and lack of battle experience ensured that Pétain was not promoted.

On the outbreak of war, with all experienced soldiers needed at the front, the 58-year-old Pétain was given command of a brigade. It was soon clear that the

Marshal Pétain in the railroad carriage that he used as his mobile headquarters during the defense of Verdun, February–December 1916.

unconventional academic was also a very able commander. His men admired his strict, no-nonsense manner, and he played an important part in the Battle of the Marne (September 1914). The following May, now commanding an army corps, he made a spectacular breakthrough during the Battle of Arras and reached the summit of Vimy Ridge, a high point that overlooked long stretches of the Western Front.

In July 1915 Pétain was given command of the Second Army and ordered to attack in the Champagne region. As he had ominously predicted, the offensive proved a costly failure. An even tougher test came the following February, when the Germans launched a massive assault on the fortifications around the town of Verdun.

Verdun was a "salient"—it lay in a bulge in the front line, surrounded on three sides by the Germans. The German commander in chief, Falkenhayn (see page 48), correctly believed that the French would defend Verdun until the end. The more men they poured into the defenses, he reasoned, the more would be killed. In this way he planned to "bleed the French army white."

French soldiers use captured German machine guns during the Battle of the Marne.

General Charles Mangin (1866–1925)

Of all the French commanders, the reputation of Charles Mangin—nicknamed "the Butcher"—was the most bloody. After drawing attention to himself at Verdun, he launched into Nivelle's 1917 offensive with great gusto. When the offensive failed to achieve breakthrough and mutiny swept through the French ranks, Nivelle fired Mangin to save his own reputation. The Butcher returned in 1918, and added to his reputation with more ferocious attacks during the Allied advance.

French firemen in Verdun, which was stricken by German shells.

Pétain, the defensive expert, was called on to hold Verdun. Although a near-impossible task, he set about it with great skill. *"Ils ne passeront pas"* ("They will not pass") was his watchword. He took personal command of the artillery, kept open a reliable supply route (the "Sacred Way"), and made sure no troops were in the front line for too long. His decisive action and his clear regard for the common soldier had a huge impact on French morale. Verdun was saved and its savior became a national hero.

Pétain's reputation rose even higher when, after further hopeless offensives, he replaced Nivelle (see page 34) as commander in chief in May 1917. When Pétain took over, the French army was on the point of collapse. Mutinies threatened to become widespread. To deal with this danger, the new commander immediately promised no more large-scale offensives. He also took a personal interest in the soldiers' welfare, as he had done at Verdun, making regular visits to the front to see for himself how things stood. In response, the army regained its morale and was able to resist the German Spring Offensive of 1918.

Between the wars, Pétain—loaded with every honor France could bestow upon him—remained one of the most admired men in the land. In 1940, however, following France's defeat by the Nazis, the 84-year-old was called back to serve his country again. This time he headed a government, based in Vichy, that cooperated with Hitler. Although the old soldier was doing what he thought best for the French people, much of his behavior appeared treacherous. After the war he was arrested, found guilty of treason, and condemned to death.

In the light of his record in World War I, Pétain's sentence was changed to life imprisonment. He was sent to a lonely island, Ile d'Yeu, several miles off France's Atlantic coast. Here, having spent his last years in solitary confinement, "the hero of Verdun" eventually died at the age of 95.

As head of France's Vichy government in World War I, Marshal Pétain (left) met with German ambassador Otto Abetz.

Commanders of the Central Powers

General Franz Conrad von Hotzendorf (1852–1925)

A close friend of Archduke Franz Ferdinand, Franz Conrad was appointed Austrian chief of staff in 1906. His outlook was openly aggressive, especially toward Serbia and Italy, and he called for immediate war after the assassination of Franz Ferdinand in June 1914. Conrad had already planned for war on two fronts, Russian and Serbian, and threw most of his forces against the Russians.

Conrad was an imaginative soldier but he lacked human and political insight. He saw things in terms of figures and lines on a map, not people. Outnumbered, he was repulsed by the Russians and failed to take Serbia until 1915 (and then only with German help). In 1915 he also planned a combined Austro-German offensive in the Gorlice-Tarnow region (now Poland), which met with some success. By this time, however, his freedom of operation was limited by the need to work closely with the more powerful German general staff.

Chief of the Austrian general staff Field Marshal Baron Conrad von Hotzendorf (right). A close friend of the assassinated heir to the throne, Archduke Franz Ferdinand, Conrad was relieved of his post in 1917.

Italy's entry into the war in 1915 on the side of the Allies presented Conrad with another problem. In the early summer of 1916, he planned to overwhelm Italy with a massive offensive. After early victories, the plan folded because troops had to be moved to the Russian front to counter the Brusilov Offensive (see page 30).

In September 1916 Paul von Hindenburg (see pages 48–51) took official responsibility for all Dual Alliance strategy. The following March Austria's new emperor, Charles I, removed Conrad from his position. He served as a field commander on the Italian front until dismissed in July 1918, after Italian successes. He spent the remaining years of his life writing his memoirs.

The Austro-Hungarian Army

Austrian commanders faced two serious problems. The first was the extended nature of the Austro-Hungarian Empire. During the war the empire fought on three fronts at the same time: Russian, Balkan, and Italian. The second problem was that its conscripted soldiers came from a multitude of backgrounds, including Austrian, Hungarian, Czech, Slovak, Croatian, Serbian, Polish, and Ukrainian. Under the pressure of defeat, army units tended to identify with their homeland rather than with their emperor.

This way, officer: Austrian soldiers in the Balkans confirm their position with local peasants.

Field Marshal Paul von Hindenburg
(1847–1934)

As his full name—Paul Ludwig Hans Anton von Beneckendorff und von Hindenburg—suggests, Hindenburg came from an old aristocratic family. His early career was typical of many men of the Prussian "Junker" (officer) class: He entered the army while still a youngster of 11 and served until the age of 65. During this time he saw action in the triumphant Seven Weeks' War with Austria (1866) and the Franco-Prussian War (1870–1871). In 1911, after long and honorable (but not very remarkable) service to his country, he retired.

Hindenburg (right) and Ludendorff, the pairing that brought Germany victory in the east and came close to breaking through in the west in the spring of 1918.

Three years later, Hindenburg was called back into the army and asked to take command of the German Eighth Army. His appointment was partly to provide a respectable senior figure beneath whom his second-in-command, the younger and more able General Erich Ludendorff (1865–1937), could operate (see pages 54–59). This was the beginning of the highly effective Hindenburg-Ludendorff partnership, with the older man as the figurehead, that lasted to the end of the war.

The new team's first task was to halt the invasion of East Prussia by two Russian armies. This was brilliantly achieved at the battles of Tannenberg and Masurian Lakes (August–September 1914), after which Hindenburg was promoted to field marshal and given command of the entire Eastern Front. Working closely with Ludendorff, he inflicted a series of defeats on the Russians during 1915 but never managed to come up with the sweeping breakthrough he hoped for. After General Falkenhayn's failure to

General Erich von Falkenhayn (1861–1922)

In 1913 Falkenhayn was Prussia's minister of war. After Moltke's defeat at the Battle of the Marne (September 1914), he also became chief of the German general staff. This made him, for a time, the single most powerful military leader of the entire war. However, disagreements with Hindenburg and the exhausting failure to capture Verdun cost him his high position. He was steadily demoted and ended the war commanding a garrison in Lithuania.

Caught in the crossfire: buildings damaged in the Battle of Tannenberg (August 1914), in which the Germans overwhelmed the advancing Russians.

take Verdun (see panel) in 1916, Hindenburg was put in overall command of all the armies of the Dual Alliance (of Austria and Germany). His enormous power and prestige now rivaled that of the kaiser. For the final two years of the war, it is said, Germany was run by the Hindenburg-Ludendorff "military dictatorship." The junior partner, however, was the real power behind the scenes. The influence of the military increased still further when, prompted by Hindenburg and Ludendorff, the kaiser dismissed Chancellor Bethmann Hollweg in July 1917 (see page 26).

Verdun

The Battle of Verdun, which ruined Falkenhayn's reputation and brought Hindenburg to supreme power, was reported in a German newspaper as:

"…not a battle at all. It is hell. A man needs a devil in him to be able to survive it. No human beings can be expected to tear away whole rows of barbed wire and escape the snares of all sorts and the pitiless machine guns. The [German] attacking forces have only death, carnage, and horror before them."

Cited in David Mason, *Verdun*

49

The strategy that Hindenburg gave his name to involved (1) forcing peace terms on Russia, (2) stepping up the blockade of Great Britain, and (3) holding a firm defensive line on the Western Front (named the "Hindenburg Line"). Although the first and third strands of this strategy were successful, they were undone by the failure of the second.

Advance at last: British troops and tanks, equipped with trench-bridging equipment, advance toward the Hindenburg Line at Bellicourt, September 29, 1918. Despite their successes, the Allies never reached German soil.

The Hindenburg Line

The Hindenburg Line was a pre-prepared line of German defenses, about 50 miles (80 km) long, on the Western Front between Drocourt and St Quentin. The Germans began building the Line, which consisted of three rows of trenches and deep concrete blockhouses, in September 1916. When it was finished in January 1917, the Germans abandoned their positions farther forward and retired to the almost impregnable Line. The Allies finally breached it only in September 1918.

Germany's return to unrestricted submarine warfare on February 1, 1917, led to the United States' entry into the war. This in turn forced the Germans to abandon their defensive strategy on the Western Front—they had to try to end the war before American power made itself felt. When the German offensive petered out in the summer of 1918, Hindenburg knew the war was lost. However, he managed to divert blame for the military failure onto Ludendorff. He called for the armistice, advised the kaiser to abdicate, and remained in command of the German armies until July 1919. Amazingly, Hindenburg's remarkable career was still not over. In 1925 he was elected president of Germany, a position he held until his death. One of his final political acts was to appoint Adolf Hitler chancellor of Germany in 1933.

The past and the future: A Nazi election poster linking Adolf Hitler to Hindenburg, the respected war hero. The Nazis identified closely with the German army's claim that it had not been defeated in 1918.

Mustafa Kemal, often referred to as "the father of modern Turkey."

Mustafa Kemal (1881–1938)

The Turkish soldier and statesman Mustafa Kemal was named "Kemal" ("Perfect") by one of his secondary-school teachers. He would later become known as Kemal Ataturk (father of the Turks). After graduating from staff college, he joined radicals seeking to overthrow the outdated autocratic Ottoman system of government. In 1912, during the First Balkan War, he was sent to defend the vital Gallipoli Peninsula.

Gallipoli lies to the west of the Dardanelles, the narrow strip of water that links the Aegean Sea to the Black Sea. Ataturk's experience here, at one of the great crossroads of the world, would stand him in very good stead when Turkey went to war in 1914.

In 1915 the Allies were seeking to break the deadlock on the Western Front. One answer, which eventually won the support of the British and French governments, was to attack Germany and Austria from the south, through the Ottoman Empire. The exact point they chose for this offensive was the Gallipoli Peninsula.

Because of his previous experience in the region, early in 1915 Ataturk had been given command of the Nineteenth Turkish Division defending Gallipoli. Here he joined up with the German general advising the Turkish forces, Limen von Sanders. They predicted exactly where the Allied landings would come in April 1915 and brilliantly organized the Turkish resistance. Thanks to their inspired leadership, the Allies failed to gain control of the ridges that commanded the peninsula, and they withdrew their forces the following year.

From Gallipoli Ataturk was moved to the Caucasus, where he fought successfully against the Russians until their war effort collapsed in 1917. During the last year of the war, he tried in vain to halt the British advance toward Damascus. He avoided losing a battle, however, and withdrew his forces in reasonable order to Aleppo, Syria. At the end of the war, he was the only undefeated Turkish commander.

In the bloodshed and chaos that followed, Ataturk emerged as an outstanding political leader. He became the first president of the new Turkish Republic in 1924 and devoted the rest of his life to transforming his country into a modern democracy.

Enver Pasha (1881–1922)

Enver Pasha was a hero of the revolution (1908) that forced change on the Ottoman government. Unlike Ataturk, he was fiercely pro-German. As war minister, he helped bring Turkey into the war on Germany's side. He then intended to expand the Turkish Empire into the Caucasus. His badly planned campaigns against the Russians led to several disastrous defeats (notably Sarakamish, December 29, 1914). In 1918 he fled abroad and was killed fighting against the Red Army in Russia.

Allied troops and supplies landing on a Gallipoli beach, later named ANZAC (the Australian and New Zealand Army Corps) Cove. The Turkish resistance was so well organized that the landings proved a costly failure.

General Erich Ludendorff (1865–1937)

After the war Ludendorff claimed that he had been the only real commander of the entire conflict. The remark says a great deal about him. He was fiercely ambitious, highly intelligent, and blessed with enormous energy. As we shall see, however, on crucial occasions he was liable to serious errors of judgment.

As the fighting dragged on, year after year, Ludendorff came to believe in total war conducted by a single "strongman." Peace, he said, was just an interlude between wars. Such ideas were later taken up by Hitler's Nazis, of whom Ludendorff was an early leading supporter. After the war he also insisted that his armies—the German armies—had never been defeated but had been "stabbed in the back" by peace-seeking politicians. This idea, too, became part of Nazi propaganda.

In 1908 Ludendorff was placed in the department of the German army responsible for long-term planning. Here, working with the chief of the general staff, General Helmuth von Moltke (see panel), he revised the famous Schlieffen battle plan. According to the original plan, Germany would take France quickly out of the war by sweeping southwest through neutral Holland and Belgium and encircling Paris. The Moltke-Ludendorff revision abandoned the advance through Holland and strengthened the forces in the Lorraine region facing the French directly.

General Helmuth von Moltke (1848–1916)

Moltke was the nephew of the Prussian general who had smashed France in 1870–1871. The kaiser rejected the younger Moltke's belief that he was not the right man for the job and appointed him chief of the general staff in 1906. Working with Ludendorff, Moltke made crucial changes to the Schlieffen Plan. He lost control of events at the Battle of the Marne (September 1914) and was dismissed two days after it ended.

Erich Ludendorff (front right), with Hindenburg (front center) and the members of the German general staff. Ludendorff never really recovered from Germany's defeat and ended up a pacifist.

Ludendorff had never seen politics and soldiering as separate activities, and had long argued for the German army to be considerably strengthened. His campaigning so annoyed his superiors that in 1913 he was removed from the general staff. At the outbreak of war, however, he was swiftly brought back into the thick of things. First he was put in charge of supply for the German Second Army, then he was sent with Field Marshal Paul von Hindenburg to the Eighth Army in the east, as its chief of staff.

Victories over the Russians at Tannenberg and Masurian Lakes (August–September 1914) brought the Hindenburg-Ludendorff ("steel and brains") partnership to the world's attention. Ludendorff was promoted, despite the failure of his revised Schlieffen Plan in the west. During 1915 he argued for Germany to concentrate its forces in the east, to defeat Russia. The kaiser and Commander in Chief Falkenhayn rejected the idea.

Following Falkenhayn's failure at Verdun, Hindenburg (with Ludendorff as his number two) had supreme command over all German forces. Increasingly, it was Ludendorff who made the important decisions in both the military and the political sphere. He attempted to gear the entire nation —industry, agriculture, and transportation—to winning what he called a "victorious peace." For a time in 1917–1918, it looked as if he might succeed.

Revolution removed the czar of Russia in March 1917. Ludendorff then allowed Lenin and other dissidents to return to Russia to stir up more trouble. In the short term the plan worked. Torn apart by a second (communist) revolution in November 1917, Russia was forced to accept humiliating peace terms at Brest-Litovsk (March 1917). Now Ludendorff was free to concentrate on the Western Front.

Believing Great Britain had to be starved into making peace, in January 1917 Ludendorff had approved of restarting unrestricted submarine warfare. Partly as a result, the United States joined the war on

Colonel Paul von Lettow-Vorbeck (1870–1946)

Lettow-Vorbeck was the greatest guerrilla soldier of World War I. Having served in China and Southwest Africa (now Namibia) before the war, in 1914 he was put in command of the forces in German East Africa (now Tanzania). He proved an inspirational leader. For more than four years his tiny force of Germans and Africans tied down 130,000 Allied troops. Often living off the land, he carried out a series of brilliant guerrilla raids all over eastern Africa.

A painting of the Battle of Jutland, the one great naval encounter of the war. As the British lost more ships but forced the Germans back to port, both sides claimed victory.

Admiral Reinhard Sheer (1863–1928)

Sheer became famous for his submarine tactics: using surface ships as "bait" to lure warships toward waiting U-boats. In January 1916 he was given command of the German High Seas Fleet. At the Battle of Jutland (May–June 1916) he failed to divide the British Grand Fleet. However, fearing a U-boat trap, Admiral Jellicoe did not press home his advantage. Maneuvering expertly, Sheer returned safely to harbor and claimed victory since his sinkings outweighed his losses.

the Allies' side in April 1917. Although this development (and the success of convoys in cutting the U-boats' success rate) was alarming to Germany, it was not fatal. It would be at least a year, Ludendorff estimated, before the United States could raise, train, and ship sufficient troops to make an impact in Europe. By then, he thought, it would be too late—he would have won the war.

For the rest of 1917 Ludendorff's armies soaked up the incessant Allied attacks. Then, on March 21, 1918, he launched his Spring Offensive. The first attack came at the Somme, 63 German divisions driving into 26 British divisions after a 6,000-gun bombardment with shells of high explosive and poison gas. The British line buckled and pulled back. Delighted, Ludendorff ordered his men to press farther ahead than originally planned—to Amiens, the Channel ports, and even Paris.

The Allies reacted by placing Marshal Ferdinand Foch in overall command of their forces. French troops poured in to reinforce the British. Although they were 50 miles (80 km) farther back, the Allied line reformed and the Germans were stopped. Ludendorff had underestimated

"A Brilliant Achievement"

In his war memoirs Ludendorff justified withdrawing German forces into pre-prepared defensive positions in March 1917:

"The decision to retreat was not reached without a painful struggle.... The Entente [Allied] armies followed closely on the heels of our retiring forces and tried to make out that our retreat was a great success for themselves.... As a matter of fact they had not gained any military triumph.... The whole movement was a brilliant achievement on the part of both commanders and troops, and is evidence of the careful foresight and work of the German general staff."

Cited in Lyn Macdonald, *1914–1918, Voices and Images of the Great War*

The final fling: German cavalry take up their positions during Ludendorff's Spring Offensive, 1918. Since complete breakthrough never came, cavalry could not be used.

both the strength of his own forces and the ability of his enemy to regroup. Abandoning the Somme offensive, he turned his attention to Lys in Flanders.

Since it was farther south, the Allied line at Lys was driven back but did not completely break. The same happened at the Marne, where in the middle of July 1918 Ludendorff launched his final great offensive. However, unlike at the Somme and at Lys, the Allies responded with an immediate counterattack. By the beginning of August, the German advance had become a defeat. The Spring Offensive cost Ludendorff well over half a million men, more than the German army could withstand.

That fall it retreated steadily toward Germany. As his allies (Austria-Hungary, Bulgaria, and Turkey) capitulated, Ludendorff urged the kaiser to seek peace terms. The general, now close to collapse, was receiving psychiatric treatment. When he heard the harsh terms the Allies demanded for a cease-fire, he rejected them and called for the army to fight on.

The political will for further bloodshed was not there. Ludendorff offered his resignation on October 26, 1918, and the kaiser accepted it. (To Ludendorff's intense anger, however, the kaiser refused to accept Hindenburg's.) Exhausted and wholly shattered in spirit, Ludendorff fled in disguise to Sweden. After the war he became one of the most prominent early Nazis and joined Hitler's attempted rising at Munich in 1923. He was acquitted of treason at the time and later served as a Nazi member of the Reichstag, 1924–1928. In his final years he became increasingly eccentric, dying a pacifist two years before Germany entered a second world war.

59

Date List

1848	Franz Josif becomes emperor of Austria.
1861–1865	American Civil War.
1866	Prussia defeats Austria in the Seven Weeks' War.
1870–1871	Franco-Prussian War.
1871	**January** German Empire proclaimed at Versailles. **May** Treaty of Paris. France cedes Alsace and Lorraine to Germany.
1877–1878	Russo-Turkish War.
1879	Austro-German Dual Alliance formed.
1888	Wilhelm II becomes emperor of Germany.
1899–1902	Anglo-Boer War.
1904	Anglo-French *entente cordiale*. Russo-Japanese War (to 1905).
1905	Schlieffen Plan drawn up.
1906	Franz Conrad von Hotzendorf appointed Austrian chief of staff.
1907	Anglo-Russian *entente*.
1909	Theobald von Bethmann Hollweg becomes chancellor of Germany.
1912	Woodrow Wilson elected president of the United States.
1914	**June 28** Archduke Franz Ferdinand assassinated in Sarajevo, Bosnia. **August** War spreads across Europe. Paul von Hindenburg and Erich Ludendorff defeat Russians at Tannenberg. **September** Hindenburg and Ludendorff defeat Russians at Masurian Lakes. German advance stopped at the Battle of the Marne. Erich von Falkenhayn replaces

Helmuth von Moltke as German commander in chief.
October First Battle of Ypres **(to November)**. Turkey joins Central Powers (Germany and Austria).
November Hindenburg given full command on the Eastern Front. Russian advances in Galicia.

| 1915 | **February** Germany begins unrestricted submarine warfare **(to September)**.
April Allies land at Gallipoli but fail to advance beyond the coast.
May Italy joins Allies. Germans making gains on Eastern Front.
August Germans capture Warsaw in Poland. Czar Nicholas II takes command of Russian armies.
September Bulgaria joins Central Powers.
December Joseph Jacques Césaire Joffre becomes French commander in chief. Douglas Haig replaces Sir John French as British commander in chief. |
| 1916 | **February** Falkenhayn begins attack on Verdun **(to December)**. Henri Philippe Pétain ordered to defend Verdun.
May–June Battle of Jutland.
June General Aleksey Brusilov begins his offensive on the Eastern Front **(to September)**. Kitchener drowned.
July Haig begins the Somme |

60

offensive **(to November).**

1916 **August** Romania joins Allies. Hindenburg replaces Falkenhayn as German commander in chief.
October Lawrence of Arabia begins working with Arab guerrillas.
November Woodrow Wilson reelected to his second term as U.S. president.
December. Lloyd George replaces Herbert Henry Asquith as British prime minister.
Joffre replaced by Robert Nivelle as French commander in chief.

1917 **January** Zimmermann telegram intercepted.
February Germans begin to fall back to Hindenburg Line. Germans reintroduce unrestricted submarine warfare.
March Nicholas II abdicates after revolution in Russia. Germany and Russia sign Treaty of Brest-Litovsk.
April 6 United States declares war on Germany.
April Nivelle's offensive on Western Front.
May Convoys introduced. Pétain replaces Nivelle as French commander in chief.
June First American troops land in France.
July Brusilov dismissed. Bethmann-Hollweg dismissed. Haig begins Third Battle of Ypres—Battle of Passchendaele **(to**

November).
October Italians defeated at Caporetto.
November Communist revolution in Russia. Georges Clemenceau becomes prime minister of France.

1918 Civil War in Russia (to 1921).
January Wilson puts forward his "Fourteen Points."
March Ludendorff begins his final offensive. Ferdinand Foch appointed as supreme commander of Allied forces.
July Ludendorff's last offensive, followed by Foch's first counterattack.
August Foch launches Amiens Offensive.
September John Joseph Pershing's offensive at St. Mihiel. Foch launches Meuse-Argonne Offensive.
November Kaiser Wilhelm II abdicates.
November 11 Armistice declared. World War I ends.

1919 **January** Paris Peace Conference opens.
June Treaty of Versailles signed.
October Wilson suffers a stroke.

1922 Lloyd George resigns as British prime minister.

1925 Hindenburg elected president of Germany.

1939 **September** Nazi Germany invades Poland; start of World War II.

Glossary

abdicate to give up a throne out of choice.

AEF American Expeditionary Force, the U.S. army in Europe.

Allies Russia, France, Great Britain, Italy, the United States, and the countries that fought alongside them in World War I.

aristocratic belonging to an old, privileged family with a title, such as "duke."

armaments weapons of all sorts.

arms race attempt by two or more countries to try to outdo each other by building up the size of their armed forces.

artillery heavy guns.

attrition wearing down the enemy.

Austria-Hungary Dual Monarchy of Austria and Hungary, joined in 1867.

autocratic all-powerful.

blockade cutting off of supplies.

blockhouse concrete shelter.

Boers settlers in South Africa originally descended from the Dutch.

breech-loading gun modern gun that is loaded from the end nearer the firer rather than at the other end (muzzle loader).

brigade army unit of about 1,000 men.

cabinet leading members of a government.

censorship government control of all public information, such as the contents of newspapers, and the cutting out of anything the authorities believe might help the enemy or lower morale.

Central Powers Germany, Austria-Hungary, and Turkey.

chancellor German prime minister.

chancellor of the exchequer Great Britain's finance minister.

chief of staff top military commander. (Also chief of general staff or imperial general staff.)

coalition government made up of members of more than one political party.

colony overseas possession of an empire.

commander in chief head of the army, the leading general.

communist believing in an all-powerful government that owns most things and sees that wealth is distributed equally among all people.

Congress the group of elected American officials that makes the laws.

conscript someone obliged by law to join the armed forces.

Conservative party British political party that in the early 20th century believed in the British Empire and opposed radical ideas.

constitution laws and customs by which a country is governed.

convoy many merchant ships traveling together under the escort of warships.

corps large body of troops.

counteroffensive attack launched soon after an enemy attack.

deadlock a situation in which no side has an advantage and neither will give in.

defeatism believing that one's own side will lose.

democracy government by the people or their elected representatives.

Democratic party one of the two main American political parties, the other being the Republican party.

dictatorial unwilling to listen to the advice or opinions of others. Tyrannical.

diplomacy high-level contact between states.

dissident not in agreement with the government.

division army unit of about 10,000 men.

dreadnought fast, heavily armored battleship, after HMS *Dreadnought* (launched in 1906).

Dual Alliance alliance between Austria and Germany, 1879.

Dual Monarchy combined crowns of Austria and Hungary.

Eastern Front battlefront between the Central Powers and Russia.

empire many territories, sometimes in different parts of the world, under the same government.

entente agreement.

field marshal highest rank in the army.

figurehead person in a position of respect but without power.

foreign policy state's policy toward other states.

foreign secretary minister responsible for relations with other countries.

front line the area where two opposing armies meet.

garrison troops in a regular base.

general staff generals and other officers responsible for army organization, planning, and strategy.

Grand Fleet Great Britain's main battle fleet in World War I.

guerrillas soldiers who fight by using ambush and terrorist tactics.

hemophilia disease that prevents the blood from clotting.

High Seas Fleet Germany's main battle fleet in World War I.

imperial of an empire.

Jesuit order of Roman Catholic priests.

Junker a group of upper-class Prussian families that provided the army with its officers for generations.

kaiser German emperor.
Labour party British political party that at the time of World War I believed in social reform.
Liberal party British political party that in the early 20th century favored widespread social reform.
mediator go-between.
minister person responsible for an area of government, such as war or finance.
morale mood or spirit of a people at war.
munitions provisions of war, such as shells.
mutiny refusal by members of the armed forces to obey their commanders.
National Assembly France's law-making body.
offensive a large-scale attack.
Ottoman official name of the Turkish empire.
outflank to go around a line of enemy troops.
pacifist against war as a principle.
Parliament lawmaking body of Great Britain.
premier political leader or head of state.
prime minister leading or chief minister, the head of government.
propaganda political information (often false) that gives only one point of view.
province region of a country or empire having its own local government.
provisional temporary.
Prussia area of Eastern Germany around Berlin.
Reichstag the lower house of the German government.
reparations payment by the losing side to the victors after a war, to make good the losses.
revolution complete, swift, and permanent change.
salient bulge in the front line that extends into enemy territory.
Senate the upper house in many governments.
social reforms changes in laws or government policy that improve people's lives in areas such as health and housing.
stalemate position where no side appears to be able to win.
supply line the route along which supplies are brought to an army.
tactician someone skilled at planning and carrying out maneuvers.
theater of war area where fighting takes place.
total war war that involves all of a country's resources and people.
Welfare State idea that the state (the government) should see that everyone has the basics of life, such as housing, health care, and education.
Western Front front lines between the Allies and the Central Powers in France and Belgium.

Sources and Resources

Further Reading

Allan, Tony. *The Causes of World War I (20th Century Perspectives)*. Chicago, IL: Heinemann Library, 2002.

Blohm, Craig. *Leaders and Generals (American War Library World War I)*. San Diego, CA: Lucent Books, 2001.

Dolan, Edward F. *America in World War I.* Brookfield, CT: Millbrook Press Inc., 1996.

Murphy, Donald. *World War I (Turning Points in World History)*. San Diego, CA: Greenhaven Press Inc., 2002.

Ross, Stewart. *Causes and Consequences of World War I.* New York: Raintree Steck-Vaughn Publishers, 1998.

Other Sources

Atkins, Nicholas. *Petain.* New York: Longman Publishing, 1997.

Bourne, John. *Who's Who in World War One.* New York: Routledge, 2001.

Clark, Alan. *The Donkeys.* North Pomfret, VT: Pimlico, 1991.

Grigg, John. *Lloyd George: War Leader.* New York: Allen Lane, 2001.

Keegan, John. *The First World War.* North Pomfret, VT: Hutchinson, 1998.

Lawrence, T. E. *Seven Pillars of Wisdom.* New York: Penguin Books, 2000.

Lieven, Dominic. *Nicholas II.* North Pomfret, VT: Pimlico, 1994.

Macdonald, Lyn. *1914–1918 Voices and Images of the Great War.* New York: Penguin Books, 1991.

Macdonald, Lyn. *They Called it Passchendaele.* New York: Penguin Books, 1993.

Massie, Robert K. *Nicholas and Alexandra.* North Pomfret, VT: Pimlico, 1991.

Van der Kiste, John. *Kaiser Wilhelm II.* New York: Sutton Publishing, 1999.

Places to Visit

The National Air and Space Museum
National Mall at 7th and Independence Ave., S.W.
Washington, D.C. 20560

The Stars and Stripes Museum/Library Association, Inc.
17377 Stars and Stripes Way
Bloomfield, MO 63825

Index

Numbers in **bold** type refer to illustrations.

© 2002 White-Thomson Publishing Ltd.